THE SILK ROAD

THE SILK ROAD

Photography by Jacky Yip, China Photo Library
Text and captions by Judy Bonavia

Chartwell Books, Inc.

Published by Chartwell Books, Inc.,
A Division of Book Sales Inc., 110 Enterprise Avenue,
Secaucus, New Jersey 07094 and The Guidebook
Company Limited, The Penthouse, 20 Hollywood
Road, Central, Hong Kong

Text and captions by Judy Bonavia

Photography by Jacky Yip, China Photo Library.
Additional photographs by Chan Yuen Kai (50 top, 69,
78—79); Peter Fredenburg (17, 43, 50 bottom, 71 bottom
right, 72—73, 74—75 left); Kazuyoshi Nomachi (2—3, 40);
Cary Wolinsky (8-9); Zhong Ling (5, 41 left/top and
bottom right, 42).

Designed by Joan Law Design & Photography
Color separations by Rainbow Graphic Arts Co., Ltd.
Jacket color separations by Sakai Lithocolour
Printed in Hong Kong

ISBN: 1-55521-284-0

Title spread
The sand dunes of Mingsha near Dunhuang are popular with tourists, who either make the very arduous trek on foot or camelback. Legend tells of two armies buried beneath the sands whose war drums can be heard when the wind sweeps across the dunes. Marco Polo called them the 'rumbling sands'.

Right
Natural pigments of blue, green, black and red were the preference of the artists who created the wall murals and statues in the Buddhist cave monasteries along the Silk Road. They show a combination of Indian, Chinese and Greek styles in portraying the human body, a reminder that Xinjiang was the ancient meeting place of cultures.

Pages 6-7
The pavilioned watchtowers of the Jiayuguan Pass in the Great Wall stand on the turreted ramparts of this 14th-century fortification. The pass was built to keep out the roving Mongol armies after the fall of the Yuan Dynasty. All caravans passed through its portals. Jiayuguan was the last real contact with their motherland that Chinese exiles encountered, and many marked their passage with poignant verses scratched into its walls.

Pages 8-9
According to archaeological evidence, the art of sericulture or silk-making in China is at least 6,000 years old. From the Zhou Dynasty (1122—770 BC) on, annual court rituals were held to commemorate the Goddess of Silk, Lei Zu. It was not until the fifth century AD that Roman Byzantium learnt the art. Sericulture is a lucrative side-line occupation for peasant families in China, as a single cocoon will yield up to 1,000 metres (1,094 yards) of silk thread.

Pages 10-11
In summer, Kazakh herdsmen use the verdant pasturage along the shores of Lake Sailimu to graze herds of camels, horses, sheep and cattle. Each July the lakeside is sprinkled with felt yurts as thousands of Kazakhs gather for horse races, wrestling and popular mounted games such as 'buzkashi' (a ferocious game with a sheep's carcass as a ball) and 'girl chasing', when young unmarrieds pursue each other in a playful game of catch-a-bride.

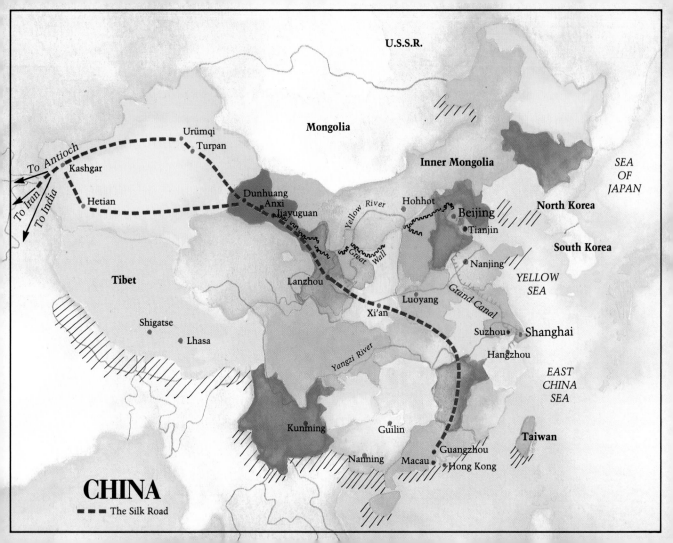

U.S.S.R.

Mongolia

Inner Mongolia

SEA
OF
JAPAN

To Antioch

Urümqi
Turpan

Kashgar

Hohhot

Beijing

North Korea

To Iran

Hetian

Dunhuang
Anxi
Jiayuguan

Yellow River

Tianjin

South Korea

To India

Great Wall

Nanjing

YELLOW
SEA

Tibet

Lanzhou

Luoyang

Grand Canal

Xi'an

Shigatse

Lhasa

Suzhou

Shanghai

Hangzhou

EAST
CHINA
SEA

Yangzi River

Kunming

Guilin

Taiwan

Nanning

Macau

Guangzhou

Hong Kong

CHINA

----- The Silk Road

INTRODUCTION

HISTORY and enigma haunt the lonely oases of the ancient Silk Road. For each traveller it has different associations — some relive the travels of Marco Polo, some the adventures of the 19th- and 20th-century explorers and archaeologists, for others it is a Buddhist pilgrimage.

For centuries the political turbulence and geographical isolation of Chinese Central Asia fed curious Western minds with an increasing fascination for the region's secrets. The pieces of the tantalizing jigsaw puzzle were snippets of miscellany gleaned from superstitious but unobservant caravan merchants whose weather-worn eyes were more set upon profit and survival than on cultural observation.

Though the term 'Silk Road' dates only from the 19th century — coined by German geographer Baron von Richthofen — the route itself dates back at least to the second century BC when significant trade opportunities between the Chinese and Roman Empires were first created by the Chinese emissary-extraordinaire, Zhang Qian. His overtures to the kingdoms of the Western Regions — Ferghana, Sogdiana, Bactria, Parthia and Northern India — opened trade routes that traversed some of the most inhospitable terrain on the face of the earth.

Little was it realized then that these routes, marked only by the bones of perished men and animals, would be the conveyors of knowledge which was to transform profoundly forever the cultures of East and West. To the West came first silk — that diaphanous product of the *bombyx mori* caterpillar or silkworm — which won the hearts of Roman citizens who bedecked themselves in 'glass togas' of silk from 'the land of Seres'. The insatiable demand was to deplete the coffers of the Byzantine empire by the fourth century AD. To the East came the art of wine-making and the first grape-vines.

From China came the art of paper-making and moveable-type printing, porcelain and gunpowder. From the West came the art of glazing and glass-making. From Central Asia come oils of frankincense and myrrh, horses, indigo dyes, walnuts and peaches. From India came cotton, pepper and fragrant sandalwood. The list was to grow and grow.

China benefitted philosophically as well as in the arts and sciences. The Road brought Indian Buddhism, Byzantium's Nestorianism and Manichaeism, Persia's Zoroastrianism and Arabia's Islam.

For today's traveller it is not only the weight of history that makes the Silk Road intriguing. Whether driving up over the mountains, from Pakistan along the Karakoram Highway, heart in mouth, bound for Kashgar and points east, or whether setting off from sedate Xi'an, the ancient imperial capital city then called Changan, by train or plane for points west, a diversity of scenery, customs and sites is in store.

Xi'an, capital of Shaanxi Province, is today a modern functional city with broad avenues, stark apartment houses and plush joint-venture hotels. But it still staunchly harbours relics of its more glorious past, such as ancient city walls and temples and pagodas from its period of greatest flourishing, the Tang Dynasty (AD 618 — 907). During this period its palaces rang with the sound of Central Asian music from Kucha, dancers from Samarkand and Tashkent and the court often dressed in Turkish costume. Its markets were thronged with foreign merchants and imported luxuries, and its monasteries housed scholarly monks bent over translations of Sanskrit Buddhist scriptures. Today the city has remains of an earlier period, those of the Emperor Qinshihuangdi, who unified China in the 3rd century BC and whose partially excavated tomb of terracotta warriors is one of the wonders of our civilized world.

Moving northwest along the Road between Xi'an and Lanzhou, the landscape is one of yellow loess soil cliffs; peasants live in caves in order not to waste cultivable

Pages 12-13
Sunset over the Baghrash Kol (Bositeng Lake) near Korla in Xinjiang. The vast lake offers a meagre source of income to Mongol fishermen during the summer months. The 1,000-square-kilometre (622-square-mile) lake is the source of the Peacock River (Konche Darya) which flows through the northern sands of the Taklamakan Desert.

The foothills of the Tianshan Mountains are clad with forests where horseriding Kazakhs and Kirghiz roam.

Rock stratification shows the complex geological processes that have formed the desert and mountains.

land for growing sorghum (a tropical cereal grass) and wheat. Here local customs and traditional arts and crafts thrive.

Lanzhou, in Gansu Province, already presages the odd feeling of a frontier town. Although Chinese comprise 97 percent of the population, the numerous Muslim Hui people here have distinctive Arab features reflecting their origins. Turkic, Tibetan and Mongol faces can also be discerned amongst the pressing crowds in this Yellow River city. Hydroelectric dams below and above the city now block the river's flow, limiting the navigability of a waterway, where once inflated animal-hide rafts were the most common form of water travel.

To the south of Lanzhou, atop steep rutted canyons, the Dongxiang minority people, of Mongolian descent, tend meagre crops of barley, wheat and potatoes. And further beyond lie grasslands, fragrant with the scent of summer wildflowers, roamed by Tibetan herdsmen who congregate at the magnificent Labrang Monastery for the festivals of their religious calendar.

The narrow corridor of Gansu Province (also known as the Hexi Corridor), hemmed in on the north by desert vastness and on the south by mountain ranges (what are now Inner Mongolia and Qinghai Province respectively), was home to early nomadic tribes of Turkic and Indo-European ancestry. They were driven from their grazing lands by cruel Xiongnu tribes. The towns along the Gansu Corridor flourished during the heyday of Silk Road trade. Caravanserais served the long caravans travelling east and west. Chinese dynasties, at war with 'barbarians' beyond the Great Wall, maintained imperial pastures in the corridor, bartering silk and tea for herds of horses. Muslim revolts swept through the region late last century, burning to the ground much of ancient architectural interest.

The Great Wall no longer represents the frontier of the country, but the grand and solitary Ming-Dynasty (AD 1368 — 1644) fort of Jiayuguan ('The Greatest Pass under Heaven') still marks a geographical border. Standing on its ramparts, one can see the powerful contrast in landscapes: to the west a horizon of empty, stony desert, to the east the soothing green of tree groves and cultivated fields. Little wonder that China's political and criminal exiles scratched words of fear and sadness upon its walls as they passed through. Walking along the eroded and broken stretches of the Great Wall fills one with loneliness, excitement and a sense of destiny.

Some geographers maintain that the small town of Anxi, to the northwest of Lanzhou, is situated at the very heart of Asia. Now no more than a lunch stop for long-distance bus passengers, it stands at the junction of major Central Asian trade routes.

Caravans bound for the Black Sea followed the Road from Anxi for Hami, travelling north of the Heavenly Mountains, westwards to Yining and onwards into what is now Soviet Central Asia, north of Lake Issikul.

Caravans for Kashgar wound their way southwards from Anxi to Dunhuang, where merchants exchanged horses for camels and purchased supplies. They faced the impassable sand dunes of the waterless Taklamakan Desert, that straddle the direct line to Kashgar, and form a barrier at which even birds are forced to change course. To circumnavigate this natural obstacle, the caravan route bifurcated.

The more favoured Northern Silk Road headed northwest to Turpan, south of the Heavenly Mountains and along the oasis towns by the northwestern fringes of the desert to Kashgar. The Southern Silk Road set a course hard west to Loulan, then southwest through the oases of Ruojiang, Quemo, Niya and Khotan to join with the Northern route at Kashgar. The first 30 days of this journey were the worst. Marco Polo recounts the hardships and superstitions that stalked this leg: 'All the way through the desert you must go for a day and a night before you find water...there are some who, in crossing the desert, have seen a host of men coming towards them and, suspecting that they were robbers, have taken flight; so, having left the beaten track and not knowing how to return to it, they have gone hopelessly astray...even by daylight men hear these spirit voices, and often you fancy you are listening to the strains of many instruments, especially drums, and the clash of arms...'

Much of Xinjiang Province's desert region (site of the Taklamakan) is stony and is called *gebi* in Chinese, not to be confused with the Gobi Desert in Mongolia. Only small lizards scurry about the wind-driven sand piles at the base of the camel thorn bushes. The overall greyness of the expanse is deceiving, for the stones are multi-hued — black, green, red, white and aubergine. As the wind whips the sand into funnels of twirling whirlwinds, they seem to dance like ghosts across the surface of the desert.

The heaving dunes of sand of the Taklamakan, undulating over 350,000 square kilometres (135,100 square miles), ripple to the whims of the prevailing winds, perhaps recalling the lake that lay here more than 15 million years ago. The desert's Turkic name is quite frank — 'to enter is never to leave'.

The Tarim River, which is fed by the Khotan and Yarkand Rivers and whose source lies in the towering Kunlun Mountains, flows around the northern rim of the Taklamakan and empties itself into the marshes of Lake Lopnor. Along the Tarim's shores a narrow strip of dense thicket is home to wild boar, bactrian camels and even red deer, while starlings, woodpeckers, owls and sparrows cry in the reeds and poplars.

A highly organized camel expedition is necessary to penetrate even briefly the Taklamakan Desert, so the tourist must settle for the high sandy dunes around Khotan and Dunhuang to experience the exhaustion of a desert trudge. At Dunhuang's miraculous Crescent Lake — 'The skill of man made the Caves of the Thousand Buddhas, but the hand of God fashioned the Lake of the Crescent Moon' goes a local saying — the sand dunes rumble like drum-rolls when the wind sweeps across them. Legend tells of two embattled armies buried during a sandstorm a millennium ago. Perhaps the most spectacular view of the Taklamakan Desert is from the air on flights between Khotan and Urumqi.

Xinjiang Province covers 1.65 million square kilometres (636,900 square miles) — an area almost as large as the combined territory of France, Italy, Germany and Spain. One of its prefectures alone is the size of the state of California. It is a land of contrasting beauty: pine-studded mountain pastures, searing deserts, giant glacial slopes, empty blue lakes and eroded limestone pinnacles.

The province's mountain ranges mark long strategic international boundaries. The Altai Mountains to the north border the Mongolian People's Republic. The southwards sweep of the Heavenly Mountains divides China from the neighbouring Soviet Socialist Republics. The massive Pamirs line the frontier with Afghanistan, and on the other side of the Karakorams lies Pakistan.

Xinjiang's lakes are vast and empty. Around the shores of Lake Salimu north of Yining, nomadic herdsmen tend camels, horses and cattle during the summer. Outside Turpan lies the salt-encrusted Lake Aidin which, at 154 metres (492 feet) below sea level, is the lowest basin in the world and unquestionably the most dismal! The one square kilometre (just over a third of a square mile) of the Baghrash Kol (Lake Bositeng) is fished during the summer months by Mongol fishermen and the adjacent mini-lake is perhaps most distinctive for the water-lilies smothering its surface.

Thirteen nationalities share this varied landscape. The earliest inhabitants were Indo-Europeans who occupied the rich oases and the Wusun, the ancestors of the nomadic Kazakhs. The Uygurs, the largest minority group, first came to Xinjiang around the ninth century and now number close to six million.

The Uygurs are descendants of Turkic tribes from lands south of Lake Baikal in Russia. Moving into the Xinjiang Region, they adopted Manichaeism and Buddhism before slowly converting to Islam after the tenth century. As they occupied the oasis

Wild flowers and butterflies decorate the hillsides and forests.

A lavender field near Yining provides a source of income for the local people and makes fragrant the surrounding meadows and woods.

An Uygur family enjoys a traditional welcome meal — called a Dastarkhan — *of pilau,* nan, *side dishes and fresh fruit. A cloth is laid upon the ground and the family and guests seat themselves around it. A beautiful hand-woven carpet covers the arch with delicate Islamic tracery.*

Multiple rows of Buddha figures have been disfigured by Muslim fanatics, who consider it sinful to portray the human face.

towns, the control of the trade routes naturally fell to them. They were accomplished agriculturalists and administrators and many held high office during the Tang and Yuan Dynasties.

Uygurs dominate the agriculture of southern Xinjiang and form a majority of the population in cities such as Turpan, Kucha, Kashgar and Khotan. They tend fields of cotton, maize, wheat, vegetables and melons, vineyards and orchards of apricots, peaches, pears and plums. They are famed for their silk and their carpets and as traders.

In dress the Uygurs mix the contemporary with the traditional. Modern clothing for women is usually a blouse and skirt with unglamorous thick brown stockings which are worn the year round. Many women, however, still prefer to wear traditional, smock-like dresses of variegated colours, preferably made from tie-dye, hand-spun *ai-de-lai* silk. Few of the women are seen these days embroidering the traditional Uygur *dopa* hats; now these are mostly mass produced and have lost regional variety. Nevertheless, the Islamic custom of covering women's heads is adhered to strictly, regardless of whether it is a *dopa*, a headscarf or, increasingly, a veil that is used. The men cut more dashing figures, sporting high black leather boots and sashed three-quarter-length coats, a *dopa* or fur hat — regardless of the season.

The hub of Xinjiang's economy is Urumqi, the provincial capital. In the days of the Silk Road, it was little more than a garrison station for Chinese troops. Now Urumqi is a city of anomaly: glass and concrete skyscrapers stand alongside elegant Russian mansions with moulded stucco façades and columned porticos that were built before the Sino-Soviet split of 1960. Only in the dusty, unpaved back streets are the overcrowded living conditions of single-storey, chipped, mud houses apparent. Like that in other big Chinese cities, Urumqi's modern housing construction lags behind demand.

In the city of Yining close to the Soviet border, it is the Russian architecture that predominates. This is hardly surprising given that until 1949 it was a Soviet town in all but name. A few hundred Russians still live in this region, descendants of 18th-century settlers.

Buddhism began to spread across the desert regions from Northern India during the first century BC. The rich Indo-European trading communities created treasure houses of Buddhist sculpture, painting and literature. Whole kingdoms took Buddhism as their religion, dedicating temples to their belief. These, and the cities which surrounded them, have long been buried beneath the sands and survive only as archaeological sites. It is in the hand-hewn caves of devout monastic communities that we can still appreciate the beauty of the period and marvel at the miracle that such fragility should have survived at all.

Many 'Thousand Buddha Caves' are to be found along the entire length of the Silk Road — Maijishan, Binglingsi, Mogao, Bezeklik and Kizil are a few of them. Merchants and travellers donated money to these quiet refuges in grateful thanks for having survived the hazards of the journey and seeking heavenly protection and guidance for the stage ahead. Local aristocracy, too, paid homage and contributed to the beautification of the caves.

The frescoes and statues adorning the caves are typical of an artistic style that scholars have labelled Gandharan. This clearly carries the influences of ancient Greek, Roman, Persian and Indian artistic expression. (Later, artists combined this Indo-Hellenistic style with the principles of classical Chinese painting, a combination that reached perfection in the Sui and Tang Dynasties from the sixth to tenth centuries.)

The Mogao Caves of Dunhuang contain the most complete and most stunning examples of Gandharan art. They do indeed form 'a great art gallery in the desert' to quote the missionary and traveller Mildred Cable. The richness of content of these caves alone has spawned an international academic study known as 'Dunhuangology' to research the priceless paintings, sculpture and manuscripts of the caves. The West originally heard of them during the first decade of this century when archaeologist Sir Aurel Stein was given some of the cave's exquisite silk paintings and invaluable manuscripts by the self-appointed abbot of the deserted caves.

The 'Thousand Buddha Caves' of Bezeklik in the Flaming Mountains around Turpan also have magnificent wall paintings vividly depicting the court of the Kingdom of Gaochang in the seventh century, though sadly not all have survived desecration by both foreigners and locals. The caves overlook a breathtaking panorama high above the Murtuk River gorge.

Perhaps the finest examples of Central Asian Buddhist art were once at the Kizil Caves, outside Kucha. Now only faded fragments remain — the museums of Berlin, Tokyo and Leningrad have removed the rest.

Comprehensive exploration of the numerous archaeological sites in the region is beyond the meagre budgets of the provincial museums and state cultural bureaux. Indeed, much of the significant excavation of buried cities was undertaken arbitrarily by Western explorers-cum-archaeologists such as Sven Hedin, Sir Aurel Stein, von LeCoq, Paul Pelliot and a number of Japanese expeditions at the turn of the century.

The abandoned cities of Gaochang and Jiaohe at Turpan are the most impressive. Their ruined, tamped mud-brick walls date from the seventh century AD, though the sites were founded as early as the first century BC. The sophisticated and tolerant society (in which Buddhist, Nestorian and Manichaean teachings were practised before the spread of Islam) that inhabited these cities built extensive palace and monastery complexes, residential areas and official buildings. Manuscripts in Chinese, Tibetan, Sogdian, Sanskrit, Tocharian and Uygur discovered among the ruins show the cities to have been at a crossroads of trade and culture.

Xinjiang's bazaars, as traditional as any of the dusty mediaeval Central Asian ones could ever have been, certainly do not need excavating, however. Once a week the sleepy towns along the Urumqi-Kashgar highway are transformed as floods of Uygur peasants, their donkey carts lopsided with produce, establish themselves along alleys and streets in preparation for the day's trading. Arranging piles of smooth-skinned apricots, sweet figs and bunches of 'Mare's Nipple' grapes about themselves, they squat and gossip loudly with their neighbours. Many of the sellers are women, some veiled in brown shawls, and all look after their takings in the same way — hitching up their dresses and stuffing the notes into the tops of their gartered stockings.

The sales pitch is aggressive and, in addition to selling exotic food, their wares are varied: embroidered caps, herbal medicine, sheep skins, saddle bags, felt rugs, tassled harnesses, leather boots, brown sugar lumps, bags of wool, agricultural implements, beaten tin trunks and brightly painted baby-cradles.

The heat, dust and flies never daunt the hungry who cluster under make-shift shade and partake of such local delicacies as boiled sheep's head, fatty lung with spicy sauce, rice pilau, bowls of fresh yoghurt and barbecued *shashilk*. Some Chinese dishes — cold translucent noodles and boiled stuffed dumplings — are popular too. From the bakers' deep round ovens comes the aroma of freshly baked flat *nan*, bread in different shapes and sizes, and also of popular *kao baozi* (little meat and onion pies). Tea is the favourite beverage, although cooling and medicinal fruit drinks such as mulberry and pomegranate juices also quench the thirst well. The strains of Uygur and Pakistani pop songs contribute to the din.

Away from the bazaars at Turpan, the shade under leafy poplar and fruit trees and trellised vineyards, as well as the fields of cotton and maize irrigated by *karez* (underground water channels), contribute to the town's pleasant climate. Behind high mud walls which reflect the enervating summer heat, families find refuge in the

Cupola, gate, and ornately decorated living quarters are typical examples of Islamic architecture in Xinjiang. The house and its decor are traditionally Uygur.

19

The ancient skills of carpet making and silk weaving are still carried on in villages and encampments. The nomadic Kazakhs and Kirghiz create brightly coloured and durable felt carpets made from matted wool tamped with water (top). Uygur women prefer hand-loom tie-and-dye Ai-de-lai-xi *silk for their traditional smock dresses, and lengths from Khotan are the best.*

Right
Silkworm eggs and mulberry seeds were allegedly introduced into Xinjiang over 1,000 years ago by a Chinese princess who hid them in her head-dress. The succulent leaves are plucked several times a day and fed to the voracious bombyx mori *caterpillars which are raised on large bamboo trays. The silkworm will yield finer silk if fed on the leaves of the White Mulberry. Over a one-month period, one pound of newly hatched silkworms will eat 12 tons of leaves.*

coolness of their Uygur homes — two-storey houses with carved wooden balconies, shutters and doorways.

Kashgar, like Lhasa or Khartoum, has the aura of distant inaccessibility about it. The heart of the city is situated around the Aidakh Mosque where silversmiths, bootmakers, barbers and other itinerant traders gather in front of tea shops, silk stores and hat stalls. These cater to the thousands of worshippers who arrive in truck-loads, dressed in their best clothes for Friday prayers.

Sunday's bazaar brings a more boisterous crowd into the city. It has a livestock area where macho riding skills are demonstrated by Kirghiz riders. Patient donkeys, fat-tailed sheep and irascible camels are pushed and prodded by owner and buyer alike. Shouts alert you to a herd of oncoming sheep or goats, or to handlers with their loaded carts barging through. And if anything lives on in one's memory of Kashgar, it is not so much the mullah's cry to prayer as the eternal jingling of horse bells.

The great imperial powers of Britain and Russia were locked in a cold war struggle in this part of Central Asia during the late 19th and early 20th centuries. Kashgar was one of the focuses of their confrontation. Both the British and Russian consuls here ran spy networks throughout the region from their respective diplomatic compounds, which today serve as hotels. The name of the game was knowledge and control of the high passes leading to India, and many brave military officers and surveyors lost their lives at the hands of murderous tribes in the pay of the antagonists.

The weather in Kashgar can be as treacherous as the politics. Flash flooding, from the sudden melting of snow in summer, washes away roads, bridges and railways in an instant. Sand storms that sometimes last for days constrict one's breathing. Sudden snow falls or rain squalls block mountain passes. While in the summer blazing heat makes the desert sand too hot to walk on, the winter's icy winds and temperatures crack the skin. It is perhaps the weather above all that allows us to appreciate the sheer magnitude of the journeys taken by Marco Polo, by Xuan Zang, the Chinese Buddhist monk whose pilgrimage in search of new learning took him to India and back in the seventh century, and by the countless unknown caravan traders of the Silk Road.

Preceding page
The sun low on the horizon of Xi'an picks out the exact geometric design of an ancient pagoda showing a combination of Chinese and Indian styles.

The 'Terracotta Army' of lifesize soldiers from the tomb of China's unifier, Emperor Qinshihuangdi (reigned 221–210 BC), was unearthed near Xi'an in Shaanxi Province in 1974. The ranks of soldiers, set to guard the emperor in his afterlife, include archers, infantry and cavalry. The warriors have different facial features — some have moustaches, others beards. Since many are taller than Han Chinese, it seems they represent Central Asian mercenaries. War horses stand 1.5 metres (5 feet) high. The wooden parts of weapons and war chariots have long since disintegrated, but the metal remains. Excavations at the site continue.

Devout Muslims attend their local mosque each day, but Friday prayers and special Islamic festivals draw thousands of worshippers. Muslims in China belong to the Shiite and Sunni sects. During the latter half of the 19th century, conflict between smaller, rival sects caused friction and violence amongst their adherents in Gansu Province. In Xinjiang the Huis (Chinese Muslims) and the Uygurs normally worship at different mosques.

Following page
The Maijishan Caves near Tianshui in eastern Gansu Province span some 12 centuries of religious artistic development in China. There are 194 caves, many still decorated with wall murals; the caves house some 7,000 stone and clay statues. The rectangular apertures include window spaces and earlier wooden walkway beam slots.

The unpaved streets blend with high, mud-brick walls of houses in Linxia Hui Autonomous Prefecture. Gateways of grey brick and doorways painted black and red break the monotony of yellow earth. But within, courtyards are neat and spacious, window frames are painted in gay colour and green plants ease the sun's glare.

A young mother, her head covered in a lacy velvet black cowl to conform with Islamic law (unmarried girls wear a dark green cowl), holds her child. It is the practice among Muslims in western China to arrange early marriages for their children. In the countryside girls are commonly married at 13 or 14 years of age. This young woman was married when she was 16.

These two dignified, elderly Hui (Chinese Muslim) gentlemen have been friends all their lives and pray together several times a day, either at their neighbourhood mosque or at home where they lay their prayer mats on the heated kang (bed platform) and prostrate themselves towards Mecca. They dearly wish to join the growing numbers of Muslims from China who are now permitted to make the pilgrimage to Mecca but this costs between Y7,000 and Y10,000.

An aged Uygur plays a traditional Central Asian musical instrument. Such instruments are commonly played on festive occasions, such as weddings, when, to the accompaniment of tambourines, drums and stringed instruments, Uygurs break into dance or song. Although the music of Central Asia, in particular from Kucha, had a great influence on Chinese music during the Tang Dynasty, to Chinese ears today the music is quite foreign.

Pages 34-35
Although Linxia in Gansu Province is predominantly Muslim, these Chinese worship at a Taoist temple in the hills above the city. Auspicious banners in Chinese decorate the entrance to the temple with its customary trough for burning joss sticks.

Above
Tibetan monks from Labrang Monastery in the Daxia River valley take a break from studies each summer with a three-day camp-out. They relax by playing football and singing songs; they sleep and take their meals in splendid white tents decorated with blue and white Buddhist symbols.

Left
Caravans of wool from Tibet once traversed the Daxia River valley in southern Gansu. Tibetans use yaks to plough the fields for crops of barley and wheat. To the west lies the Qinghai-Tibet plateau where the Yangzi and the Yellow Rivers rise. To the south, the swampy Songpan grasslands sweep down to Sichuan Province. In this picture a brilliant rainbow stretches across the valley after a shower of rain.

Above
The interior of this Kazakh yurt shows a woman's touch. Frequently three generations occupy a single yurt and embroidered curtains offer a modicum of privacy. Whips and harnesses are stored on the left-hand side of the yurt and cooking utensils on the right. Chests of clothing and bedding line the back of the yurt where the family sleeps. In wintertime, a stove is placed in the centre.

Left and above
This 15th-century Confucius temple (left) in Wuwei, a city in the Hexi Corridor, is a graceful complex of halls and courtyards and houses the local museum. Before the main hall hang wooden calligraphy plaques extolling Confucian virtues. The topmost reads 'The Warp is Heaven and the Woof is Earth'. Fine bronze statues grace the nearby Da Yun Temple (above).

Right
Buddhism spread along the trade routes from India and was introduced to Tibet in the third century. Here, Tibetan monks of the Yellow Hat Sect from Labrang Monastery in southern Gansu Province practise slow, whirling temple dancing. Monks perform twice a year, wearing demon deity masks, and they are accompanied by drums, cymbals and six-foot long copper horns.

The Mogao Caves of Dunhuang
represent the height of Chinese
Buddhist cave art. The first
caves were dug into the face of
the Mingsha Hills in the fourth
century, and more than 500
were hewn over the next ten
centuries. Wall murals tell the
legends of the Buddha's life and
throw light on the culture of
their time. They are in a
remarkable state of preservation.

Compassion and tranquillity are reflected in the faces of the pigmented stucco statues of the Mogao Caves of Dunhuang. Decorative motifs, typical of the ancient Buddhist kingdoms, surround the serenely sculpted head and long ear lobes which are taken as a sign of sanctity in Buddhism. A more Chinese motif is glimpsed in the two sinuous dragons on a green background above the head.

The wonder of nature is encapsulated in the tiny Crescent Lake at Dunhuang. Surrounded by 230-metre (756-foot) high dunes of shifting sands, the lake has nevertheless defied inundation. A monastery once graced its shores.

Following page
The rare Snow Lotus (Saussurea involucrata) and blue edelweiss blossom along the snowline above the Heavenly Lake in July, while on the steep, fir-clad mountain slopes, herds of Kazakh horses trample wild mushrooms, peppermint and wildflowers. The Heavenly Lake, 110 kilometres (68 miles) east of Urumqi, in the foothills of the Heavenly Mountain Range, is a popular tourist beauty spot, offering boating, horseriding and mountain-climbing.

The Emin Minaret at Turpan, built by an Uygur architect in 1777, is one of the architectural masterpieces of the Silk Road. It was begun under the reign of Emin Hodja, ruler of Turpan, and completed by his son Suleman a year later. The 44-metre-high (144-foot) tower is of sun-dried bricks and tapers in a total symmetry of geometric and flower patterns.

Preceding page
Wraiths of smoke indicate human settlement in forests at the edge of the desert. Water is present for human needs, as shown by the meandering silvery course of the river on the left.

The interior of the Emin Mosque reveals a vast prayer hall supported by unembellished wooden columns. Arched corridors on either side are carpeted with reed matting. The Turkic Uygurs moved to the Xinjiang region in the ninth century and converted to Islam a century later. They were able agriculturalists, administrators and historians who heavily influenced the Mongols. The Uygur alphabet was adopted as the basis of the Mongol written language.

The ruins of the anicent city of Jiaohe, west of Turfan (above, left), date from the Tang Dynasty (618–907). Steep river ravines formed a natural defence. The main thoroughfare is 350 metres (383 yards) long and the city complex consisted of government buildings, residential areas, a prison and a Buddhist temple at its heart. The layout, which was partially excavated in 1950, is quite distinct.

Buddhist figures can still be seen in the niches of the ruined temple area of the ancient city of Gaochang (left), 46 kilometres (29 miles) southeast of Turpan. Here in the ninth century, the Uygurs established the Kingdom of Karakhoja and it became a rich cultural centre where Buddhism, Manichaeism and Nestorianism flourished side by side. The German archaeologist von Le Coq, excavating the city in the early 1900s, found valuable manuscripts in many languages.

To protect the Silk Road from incursions by nomadic Xiongnu raiders the Han-Dynasty emperors ordered lines of tall beacon towers constructed as an advance warning system. They were garrisoned by troops who, upon sighting the enemy, set fires at night and used smoke signals during daylight hours, raising the alarm along the line of beacons to local headquarters. Beacon tower ruins are to be seen along the Northern Silk Road between Korla and Kucha.

The weathered copper-red 'Flaming Mountains' of Turpan are aptly named. As the sun blazes down the mountains appear to shimmer and move as if on fire. Their surface temperature is said to reach 80°C (176°F). It is hardly surprising that they should be the source of local folktale and myth.

Preceding page
The Thousand Buddha Caves of Bezeklik, northeast of Turpan, date from the sixth to the 14th centuries and are among the most famous in Xinjiang. The hand-hewn rock caves, high above the Murtuk River, contain fragments of wall murals, still rich in colour. Most of the statuary and frescoes were removed by foreign archaeologists at the turn of the century, while facial features have been gouged out by local Muslims over the decades.

Public notice in Uygur written in Arabic script. Arabic script has been revived in Xinjiang following a period in which an attempt was made to romanize Uygur.

Diagonal striation of rock faces reveals the history of their formation to geologists.

A herdsman leads his haughty-looking camel by the nose. His black outfit with European-style hat seems to be have been culled from miscellaneous items of clothing and is not typical of the Uygur population.

In the timeless Central Asian tradition, goods are brought to market in animal-drawn carts. At Kucha on bazaar days, the river bank serves as a parking lot. Donkeys are the principal beasts of burden and the jingle of their bell collars is heard from dawn to dusk.

Melon eating is a summer pleasure throughout China and especially in dry, enervating, desert heat. Piles of sweet Gansu, honeydew and water melons appear by the roadside tempting long-distance buses to stop for a melon-break. Nan bread comes in more than ten different shapes and sizes. Whenever Uygurs go visiting they take nan along as a present for the host.

*The Abakh Khoja Tomb in Kashgar.
Delicate tiling forms traceries of floral and
geometric designs on the tomb's cupolas
(above). The imposing blue, white and
green tiled entrance (right) is typical of the
monumental architecture of Isfahan and
Samarkand. The tomb was built in 1640
but was severely damaged in an
earthquake in 1956. Uygur women come
to the tomb to tie strips of cloth to a
window frame and offer prayers for a
child.*

Left
*The domed interior of the Abakh Khoja
Tomb in Kashgar contains the tombs of
five generations of a powerful Kashgar
family. Abakh Khoja became ruler of six
Silk Road cities during the 17th century,
and his grand-daughter is said to have
been the beloved Fragrant Concubine of
the Qing Emperor Qianlong. The tombs
are draped in colourful saddle-cloths. The
tomb is one of the holiest Islamic sites in
Xinjiang.*

Left
Beside valley streams and lakeside pastures of the Heavenly Mountains, nomadic Kazakhs make their summer home. Though the shores of Lake Sailimu abound with wild strawberries and mushrooms, the conservative Kazakhs prefer their daily diet of milky salted tea, butter and sun-dried cheese balls. Meat is eaten only on festive occasions.

Above
Herds of Kazakh horses are set free to graze in the lush green mountains during the summer, then are rounded up and taken to lower grazing grounds in winter. They are earmarked for identification. Kazakhs do not mix their animals, for individual herds of camel, horse or sheep require special handling. An average herding family will earn between Y1,000 and Y2,000 per annum.

Right
The body of a Kazakh yurt has four wooden lattice frames, a painted door, and 52 pine-wood struts that fit on to the frames and to a roof hoop. The entire skeleton is covered in layers of felt lashed down with ropes. A felt flap across the hoop acts as a skylight when pushed back. The whole yurt can be packed onto the back of several pack animals.

Left
A Kazakh housewife of Tianchi, near Urumqi.

Right
Xibo child in a traditional
*cradle. The Xibo people came as
soldiers to the Yili region from
northeast China in the mid 18th
century.*

On weekends picnickers from the provincial capital of Urumqi come in bus loads to White Poplar Gully, south of the city. Uygur families come laden with large cooking pots and take hours to prepare a rice pilau, using water from the mountain stream to cook the rice and adding apricots, almonds, mutton and spices. Kazakh families set up their yurts in the valley and offer horse rides to nervous, giggling Chinese youths.

Children of the Kazakh and Xibo nationalities share ice lollies in the Xibo county town of Cha-pu-cha-er, near Yining, western Xinjiang. The Chinese government exempted the 50 million non-Chinese nationality peoples from the 'one child only' policy applied to Han Chinese. However, as China's birthrate continues to rise, attempts are now being made to limit these minority families to two children per family.

Two young Uygur schoolgirls. Primary education begins at seven years of age and children are taught in the Uygur language. Chinese language studies commence at middle school. Travelling schools and boarding schools serve the nomadic Kazakh and Kirghiz; however, Chinese is not widely spoken in Xinjiang.

Decorative velvet skull-caps, called dopa, *are worn by Muslim men and women in Xinjiang. Embroidered in bright colours in traditional motifs, they are often beaded or couched in gold thread. They are made from four triangular pieces of cloth sewn together, shaped, and edged in black. Each region has its own style — the small blue and black disk-shaped* dopas *are worn by women from towns along the southern Silk Road.*

Weekly market days are the economic heart of the oasis towns of the Silk Road. Kashgar's Sunday bazaar draws tens of thousands of people into the city, shoving cheerfully shoulder-to-shoulder in the congestion. In the livestock area goats and sheep compete for space with horses, donkeys and camels around an open space where horesemen flamboyantly test a horse's stamina. About Y250 is the going price for a fat-tailed sheep.

Hawkers sell eggs — plain, dyed and tea-boiled. The dyed red eggs are popular at Uygur drinking parties. They are clutched in the fist and the game is to smash the shell of the opponent's egg. Nan bread is the staple diet of the Uyguirs and accompanies every meal. The unleavened dough is rolled and stamped with a pattern, then slapped onto the sides of a clay oven to bake. The mouth-watering aroma of barbecueing shashlik sticks pervades the market places of Xinjiang. The shashlik vendor sprinkles the mutton pieces with salt and cayenne pepper and shuffles them over the burning charcoal. Liver and intestines are also served in this way. The price — 10 cents a stick!

Following page
Pack animals plod along the rugged, wind-swept landscape of the Karakoram Highway between Kashgar and the Pakistan border. This is the homeland of the Kirghiz people. Camels, yaks and horses graze beside the mountain streams.

An elderly Muslim gentleman enjoys his long stemmed pipe.

Left
Systematically planted white poplar trees shade the roadways, providing a cool environment for pedestrians and draught animals alike. Tree-planting programmes have helped counteract soil erosion and protect the oases from the ever-encroaching desert. The poplar is commonly used because of its fast rate of growth and shielding foliage. It is also useful as a building material.

Pages 76-77
Khotan is traditionally famous for its carpets as well as for white jade. The local wool is thick and long and carpets are handwoven by villagers during their spare time as well as in factories. Here, Uygur women make a final inspection of a popular local design called Adial, which will be hung on a wall in some proud Uygur household.

Pages 78-79
A crescent moon deepens the mauve sky of the desert, throwing into relief two human figures atop a sand dune.